SPOT

MOTORSPORTS

STOCK CARS

by Alissa Thielges

amicus
LEARNING

track

slick

Look for these words and pictures as you read.

engine

flag

Ready? Set. Go!
The stock cars take off.
The race has begun!

IMPALA
PENNZOIL
FURNITURE ROW
IMPALA
FUSION
LOWE'S
IMPALA

track

See the track?

The cars zip around.

The longest race is 400 laps.

HOOSIER
HOOSIER
HOWE
HOOSIER

See the slick?
It is a smooth tire.
It grips the track.

slick

Pit stop!
The crew adds fuel.
They change the tires.
It takes 12 seconds!

LOGANO
SUNOCO

See the engine?
It is loud!
It uses a lot of fuel.

engine

MOOG
CHASSIS PARTS
COMP CAMS
Raybestos
The best in brakes
Edelbrock
WIX
JE
PISTONS
SUNOCO
Hoosier

CRAFTSMAN
ally
Coca-Cola
BUSCH
NASCAR

See the checkered flag?

A person waves it.

The green and blue car won!

flag

Stock cars are fast.
Do you want to see a race?

Spot is published by Amicus Learning, an imprint of Amicus
P.O. Box 227, Mankato, MN 56002
www.amicuspublishing.us

Library of Congress Cataloging-in-Publication Data
Names: Thielges, Alissa, 1995– author.
Title: Stock cars / by Alissa Thielges.
Description: Mankato, MN : Amicus Learning, [2026] | Series: Spot motorsports | Audience: Ages 4–7 | Audience: Grades K-1 | Summary: "Stock cars are the fast race cars used in NASCAR. This search-and-find book reinforces new vocabulary words with simple facts and compelling photographs to teach kindergarten readers about motorsports"-- Provided by publisher.
Identifiers: LCCN 2024050085 (print) | LCCN 2024050086 (ebook) | ISBN 9798892004862 (library binding) | ISBN 9798892005401 (paperback) | ISBN 9798892005944 (ebook)
Subjects: LCSH: Stock cars (Automobiles)—Juvenile literature. | Stock car racing—United States—Juvenile literature. | CYAC: Stock cars (Automobiles) | Stock car racing.
Classification: LCC TL236.28 .T54 2026 (print) | LCC TL236.28 (ebook) | DDC 629.228/50973—dc23/eng/20250110
LC record available at https://lccn.loc.gov/2024050085
LC ebook record available at https://lccn.loc.gov/2024050086

Ana Brauer, editor
Deb Miner, series designer
Sara Hood, book designer and photo researcher

Photos by Dreamstime/Steven Oehlenschlager, 4–5; Getty Images/Adam Pretty, 14, Sean Gardner, 3, 12–13; Shutterstock/Bruce Alan Bennett, 8–9, BW Press, 1, Fabio Pagani, 6–7, Grindstone Media Group, cover, Richard Thornton, 10–11

track

slick

Did you find?

engine

flag